I0199462

Journeys Through Prairie and Forest

Poetic Essays On the Big Questions of Life

Volume 6 — Lessons in Life for Times of Trouble

Journeys Through Prairie and Forest

Poetic Essays On the Big Questions of Life

Volume 6 — Lessons in Life for Times of Trouble

Volume Six of a Seven-Volume Set

By Paul W. Syltie

Also by Paul W. Syltie

The Syltie Family in America

The New Eden: Millennial Agriculture,
a Key to Understanding the Kingdom of God

How Soils Work: a Study Into the God-Plane
Mutualism of Soils and Crops

Understanding God's Government,
With Contrasts to Satan's Governmental System

The Three Edens, the Story of God's Universe, Earth,
and Mankind in Conflict With the Adversary

Pathways to Joy in Marriage;
Live This Way and Happiness Will Pursue You!

The Bridge to Eden, the Arduous Passage
From This Age of Chaos to the Next Age of Perfection

Journeys Through Prairie and Forest
Volume 6. Lessons in Life for Times of Trouble
by Paul W. Syltie

Publisher: IngramSpark
Copyright © 2020 by Paul W. Syltie
Editor: Paul Syltie
Editorial Assistant/Proofreader: Sandy Syltie
Photographer: Paul Syltie
Interior Design/Composition: Greg Smith
Cover Design: Greg Smith

NOTICE OF RIGHTS
All rights reserved solely by the author. The author guarantees all contents are original and
do not infringe upon the legal rights of any other person or work. No part of this book may be
reproduced in any form without the permission of the author. The views expressed in this book
are not necessarily those of the publisher.

ISBN-978-0-9980254-5-2

Printed in the United States of America

To my wonderful wife of 53 years,
and to our children and grandchildren who are the hope of the future.

Table of CONTENTS Volume 6

All photos have been taken by the author over many years.

PREFACE

WHO AM I?
WHY AM I HERE?
WHAT IS MY DESTINY?

These three questions have haunted the lives of virtually every thinking person on earth to one degree or another. They point to the very heart of our existence, and to our ultimate value, our worthiness to exist. Are we products of evolution from a primordial sea-soup, without any defined purpose in being here, or are we creations in the image of a Creator whose plan for us transcends our understanding?

The answers to these simple but profound questions dictate our decisions day by day, and ultimately the course of our careers, our friendships, our marriage partners, and how we interact within our families and communities. In many ways these answers direct our career pathway through life, and most assuredly influence our joy and fulfillment in everyday living.

I am stepping out by claiming that I have found answers — sound answers — to all three of these questions, and I am audacious enough to suggest that they are correct answers. They agree with what I understand is Truth, which is rooted in the great eternal God who made all things, and who sustains all things through the Word of His power and revelation.

But there the simplicity ends. My audacity has led to great conflicts with the realities of a corrupted earth and universe ... a corrupted human race that clings to existence day-by-day upon the whims of weather and cooperation ... neither of which often prosper to any race's benefit. We are always only weeks away from famine upon an earth that so often insults the farmer and gardener with drought, floods, heat, frost, or tempest.

As a farm boy raised close to nature, I have been so often forced from my peaceful home into the prairies and forests, the lakes, streams, and oceans of this wide earth to regain my bearings, to restore hope and gratitude, and to reset the pathway ahead when darkness threatens to overwhelm me. To leave the sterile unease of concrete jungles and flee to the forests and prairies of sanity has become a habit over the years — an addiction, one might say — and with that flight has emerged a continued stream of verbal expression that has leaped from my fingers. I cannot explain why, just that I must do it.

So ... here is a collection of some of those writings expounded over the years, some of them clearly poetic, and some of them bordering more on short essays. I attempted some way to categorize them to make them flow, but they have defied clear organization; each item is too complex to easily arrange in a coherent order. Thus, I have let them fall where they may within broad categories, and have applied pictures I have taken through the years to emphasize the messages. Photographing nature has been a passion much of my life; these images speak louder and more eloquently than my words.

I hope you enjoy these messages, and are brought into a closer association with the Creator as a result so you will be able to answer these three big questions a bit better yourself. Let us walk together through the prairies and forests of our land, our beautiful, God-given land that speaks to us so eloquently if we will but open our ears and listen.

Course in Life

If happiness seems the main course for your soul,
Then think once again: you've sought the wrong goal.

The fear of the Lord, and doing His will,
Ought always your body-mind-spirit to fill.

Death to Sin

You have the power to leave sin alone,
Out in the cold, dying, dethroned,
So let not dark evils enter your life;
Shun shady quarters, bask in God's light.

Pritchett, Texas. *None of us, even the cattle of the field, can choose to be born. We are presented to the world, and thereafter become what we are through the choices we make with the opportunities we are presented. Like this little calf and its mother, let us choose to nurture life in its fullness.*

1 Choices

Growth in Spirit

Conforming to the heavenly I cast my bread upon
The cool, clear waters flowing from Messiah's altar set
On bended rainbow, costly gemstones, far from evil's throng,
From graceless image lived in vain that this world's gods beget.

Years of toil pass fretfully upon earth's sallow face,
Of man's yoke weighing heavily to bind up nations' hope;
Caged in sin, acceptance lost, bleak loneliness, disgrace
All join as one to curse man's lot, his joyless passions grope.

As earth grows cold I find myself less able to subsist
Within its frame of trustless laws all fettered with remorse;
Instead I grow less like its bitter charms of carnal grist,
And find this breath akin to worlds above in greater force.

This world goes here … but I go there … so great the chasm bold
Between the two opposing camps: the chaos and the peace;
While man may wonder why I grasp the flowers, not the gold,
I walk the strait and light-filled path, lest life in silence cease.

Florence, Italy. *Ancient poets, artists, and writers like Dante Allighieri promoted their conception of heaven and hell to the people of their day, in the case of Dante assuming that bad people go to an ever-burning torture in hell-fire. Let us make right choices so there can be no question about the course in life we wish to take.*

DANTE ALLIGHIERI

JOURNEYS THROUGH PRAIRIE AND FOREST Poetic Essays On The Big Questions of Life

Lost Opportunity

I wished to hug my children four
This morn before they walked out the door,
But other plans got in the way;
What joy and love have slipped away.
How less a world of good is spun
By great intentions left undone.

On Forks in the Path

So often 'midst our trialsome lives the pathways fork and turn.
We wonder if the left is best, or should the right paths be
The way to just and righteous ends sojourners such as we
Should choose while tracking canyon's stream, pure water's lessons learn.

We ought to peer so carefully down each secluded way,
Noting prints of travelers whose choices were supreme,
For maybe we should likewise join their cadre 'long the stream
Of noble gents whose lives were lent to living water's quay.

Look carefully down each new path, they may be three or four,
And gather all the truth you can before that choice complete,
So blessings may abide that path, pure waters wash your feet,
That steps need not retrace themselves throughout our spirit war.

Porter, Minnesota. *The decision to have children is a marvelous choice, following the command to "Be fruitful and multiply, and replenish the earth" given to our first parents. This decision by many of our pioneer forefathers was met with the constant threat of disease, which stalked the homes of those who did not understand proper hygiene and nutrition, and led to many children dying needlessly.*

Discouragement and Rejection

No Room At the Inn

Rejected as dross, us soldiers of loss
Among worlds' dark chaotic age … but listen!
Serenades of robins, warblers, and doves
Resound 'midst day's light … joyful through life's fight
That pummels the meek — my heart cannot speak —
Righteous life cries, my bluebird friend sighs,
Yet all in vain world's plots insane
Yield black of night ere morn's red light,
Thrills pure eyes' season … release amongst reason;
Night's shroud dimly lit from minds open wide …
Undeceived,
Unleashed,
We, the wayfarers
Walking on … running …
Into light,
No place to rest,
No lair for one's head, as one Soldier said
Long ages ago.
He walked where I go;
Rejected as dross, I'm no longer lost,
'Midst intrigue's harsh wrath … I walk glassy sea's path.

Porter, Minnesota.
No better way can be found to confront discouragement and rejection than by breaking out into the natural world and absorbing the frequencies the Creator has provided, allowing the beautiful sights, sounds, and aromas of the flowers and trees, the clouds and wind, to sooth a broken and torn spirit.

Purpose

Recall the days of yesteryear
When times grow dark, a fearful potion,
As this day's dreams grow dim with fear,
While goals lose heart 'midst roiling ocean.

This short, vainglorious exercise,
In times of joy or heartache's cast,
Was meant your soul to realize
One's life in flesh can never last.

Porter, Minnesota.

*After enduring the trials
and suffering of rejection,
the brilliant light of renewed
hope will spring forth once
the lessons are learned , as
through fire and testing.*

This Present Darkness

This present night shall soon be gone,
And from its murk will wake the dawn
Into broad daylight's unveiled source,
To ravage perplexities' discourse.

Discouragement and Rejection

Rejection

This world smiles not on souls decrying sin,
Preferring men of loose and wicked means …
So if you hurt, rejected 'midst your kin,
Recall your Master first was scorned before you.

Rejected But Found

Rejected of men, even of his own kin,
He grew up in search of the ultimate love no human could ever give,
That of his true Maker and Friend …
And he found complete love in that One,
And grew in stature in spite of rejection
By a world that knew not how to erase his loneliness.

The Light Beyond

The sky is always the darkest just before the light breaks through,
And when the light breaks through its brilliance shines out to all the world
From the inner core of hope you have always maintained,
But in suffering have withheld, for hardly could you see
That depth of utter blackness worlds of deceit have thrust upon your soul,
While in patience you wait through night's horrors
For dawn's promise of peace and tranquility … and light to clearly see.

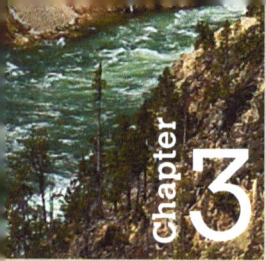

Chapter 3 Do Not Compare

Be Different

Fear not to differ from the uneasy, scurrying crowd,
For you were made for life amidst death,
Joy amidst earthly sorrow,
Faithfulness amidst apostates,
That the inundations of abundant living may stream forth from your bosom ...
Rivers of living water poured forth,
Wherein all brethren may frolic and cool themselves
Amidst the heat of Babylon's midday blistering heat.

Know Yourself

So much of unhappiness, grief and depression
Arise from imprudent comparing with others.
Presuming our neighbor's preeminence lessens
The joy we ought live hand-in-hand with our brothers.

Be careful to know your created potential,
What wonderful gifts God bequeathed to yourself,
And try not to copy vain whims existential
That crush your true image and shatter soul's health.

Yellowstone National Park, Wyoming. *Like a thundering waterfall in the midst of a dry and thirsty land, living waters will cascade into and through the heart that is bent upon seeing oneself for what he truly is, and does not compare himself with others ... a most unprofitable undertaking.*

Existence, to Live, to Be

Basic Nutrition

"Does it not make sense", said one man to his wife,
"How what goes in the mind, beef steak or swill,
Has much to do with quality in life,
As much with gastric acts as intellectual."

You are what you eat, no more, no less.
On Thanksgiving Day, all turkeys confess
That people look much less than people should be,
Less human than hoggish, more horse than manly.

Give Honor

In all things give honor to God, the High One of Israel and of all nations.
Give ear to His commandments, which never shall fail.
Serve Him, and rest secure in the shelter of His wings,
For He only is your shield and buckler,
An ever-present help.

Farson, Wyoming. *Like a flower on the desert, a child is born, grows to an adult, and passes from the scene as if in a flash. To be, to exist, is the essence of what we can comprehend in our short tenure here on the earth.*

Existence, to Live, to Be

Life So Short

Life speeds on, so fast, so fast,
Like a zephyr across the sky,
Seldom asking questions why
On fair earth this soul was cast.

For a moment sings his song
While the roses bloom and die;
Still he asks the question why
Sixty years have come and gone.

How can men in so few years
Build grim culture's nest so high,
So as eagles it might fly,
Many pains and sins he cures.

Man's course was set, I had no past,
But rest dejected, groan and sigh,
That sin should let my spirit cry
To see so few great quests I start.

What to do, you son of man,
But serve your fellow, lift him high;
Turn the quest, your self belie,
Strive to ease your brother's span.

I wept and cried as life sped on,
Tears of joy, this pain deny
If for my God each day I spy
His kingdom's plan, this world soon gone.

Looking West

Lost in life, spinning wheels, petty pursuits boring in,
Mere survival, not unfettered LIVING, casting ill dispersions across the future.
So I flee to the rustling oaks and cottonwoods, the flaming sunsets,
In search of the rite of passage I seem to have lost — or misplaced —
And I lay upon the damp, supple evening grass, staring into space.
A thunderstorm anvil looms overhead from the west; lightning stabs the earth far away.

Oh, lost soul, know you not that life begins anew each day,
And purpose, worth, and honor lie sequestered in your bosom?
Grow sophisticated, my soul, and cast out the childish seed of seeking temporal haunts;
Seek that inner throne, that dwelling place of eternal wisdom,
Which builds your house upon foundations firm, beyond man's fickle sand-prints.
Join that thunderbolt to the west, that likeness of New Jerusalem's eternal light.

Reason for Being

Tears well up whenever thoughts so range
To reasons for my presence in this strange
Forsaken realm of toil and misery,
A pilgrim and a stranger — that is me.

I did not ask to be here — born today —
A sojourner, a spirit made of clay,
Borne up by creation's mighty hand,
Saved from certain death mid sea and land.

Yet why should I, a speck in heaven's skies,
Labor, sweat, and pain as my soul cries
To once again inhabit Zion's height?
"Why am I here?' this voice cries through the night.

Too wonderful lie deep realities
Beyond the bounds of mortals' eyes to see,
Sequestered 'midst the joys of Elohim,
Reserved for brighter days and realms to be.

Sinai, South Dakota. A thunderstorm looming above the horizon leads us to contemplate the reason for our being, and the source of the power by which we exist. We are born in this time and place, live our lives, and soon pass away in the flesh ... but cannot neglect the power that will raise the dead to life once again.

Searching

Upon ageless rocks hewn by hands unseen,
Forged in images of heavenly love — yet ripped and pummeled by violence's wiles —
I sit in awe amidst astounding plans put forth amongst men and nations,
Too great for mortals' perception,
Too wonderful to unveil ... but for wisdom's light shone forth
Within the darkness of Satan's age,
To the living — to the qualified —
Even the deep things of the Eternal,
Whose quest is ever mine.

To Be …

Nothing frightens man and beast more
Than the thought of "Not to be."
Thus, all creatures fight on to love,
Sacrifice self to perpetuate their young,
That fear of death may be held at bay.

Yet, the Maker's way is, "He who finds life will lose it,
And he who would lose life for My sake will find it."
Discover success of life by forsaking all things mortal,
And live in total abandon with the One who made us all.

Unfulfilled

Where on earth's wide face must souls of flesh reside,
Years hastening towards life's final breaths, not too distant,
Cries for fulfillment yet ringing strongly within my breast,
As if nothing truly valiant or profitable has been attained.
Time, that resource above all cherished, calls out to heed her wisdom,
To consider carefully this short tenure on earth,
And use with clarity this being of God's creation
To His glory and honor in a place of His revealing,
That life will not be lived in vain,
Nor the fruits of this creation be relegated
To the weary sameness of countless souls
Bent only upon living for self, security in blending with the masses,
Never the candle that shines brilliantly in the darkness of this world's ignorance.

Germany. *As vineyards along the steep Rhine River bank cling to thin soil for survival, so we as humans ought to cling tenaciously to the purpose for which we were born, to serve the Living God who has given us life. Through strait and narrow pathways, we also can survive and thrive even in steep places as do these grapevines.*

Fight On in This Race of Life

A Rebel: That's Me!

Thrust into this world, a child of flesh,
Immersed amongst the mortals I did not choose,
What could one guess but that my wildest wish,
Should be to flee this land, this culture lose.

So flee I did, my feet ran swift and strong,
Outpacing whims of men that made this world;
They carried me far from the maddened throng,
Along a path of gold where few are hurled.

A rebel — yes! — against the gates of hell,
Yet never midst the lusts of Satan's plan,
Where most consider rebels ought to dwell,
The drug-infested, sin-sick, lustful clan.

My rebel pathways lead where few have trod,
Amongst the joy of saints not of this world,
For there the true-blue rebel's feet are shod,
With peace and hope, with loving feats unfurled.

This rebel's cause is for the just and Godly;
It leads down bumpy roads, through stormy skies,
And leaves behind the selfish, rank, and motley,
Whose claims as rebels shout their hollow lies.

A rebel: that's me,
A soldier in bonds,
To rend this world free
From false rebels' songs.

Switzerland. *The challenges we face in life can be likened to climbing a mountain: the harder the challenge, the steeper and more difficult the climb. Yet, the most demanding problems grant the most abundant fruit in the end if we will but endure them.*

Fight On in This Race of Life

Deliverance

Forget not the countless times in distress you pleaded for help,
Cried to God for deliverance when in the direst straits,
And were lifted up from calamity,
Restored to health and honor,
Redeemed from shipwreck upon the stormy seas of life.

Fleeing Mediocrity

Trapped amidst obscurity, fraught with petty tasks,
The lonely sojourner awaits his deliverance amongst the trappings reserved for
    dead and dying souls,
Not content to lose his cause amongst such fruitless avenues,
Traps laid subtly by the Deceiver, that one who masquerades as light-giver.

Extract me from the sameness, great Healer of the Breach, the tragic loss of
    mastery and accomplishment, the noose cleverly lain beneath camouflaged
    leaves and grass.
Place me on a fruitful plain beside still, deep waters, that I might fly to Your bosom
    in a quiet, private place,
After having run my course, then settled firmly on a rock upon an unsteady,
    wayward earth.

Joplin, Missouri. *Many a time there are strong obstacles placed along our pathway, sometimes natural calamities that threaten our very lives. There are no coincidences in life, so these obstacles are placed there for our ultimate edification if we will but wait patiently as we overcome, waiting for the fruits to ripen.*

Fight On in This Race of Life

I Labor

Body aging, creaking, aching, prone to rest the day away;
Mind and spirit sprightly craving that these fleshly bonds will play
Heartily upon the plains of earth's bemuddled graying trouble,
For in just a moment shall Adamic shell return to stubble.
Oh, bemoan the ravages of time's celestial rhapsody,
While I fight with all my might to fill the Maker's meed for me.

My Royal Battle

The endless sore battle I wage, each day, each moment I rage upon earth's stormy stage,
Is seeking to maximize each moment's fruits, to stand on the Rock so life's worth I may gauge
In living this life in full meaning and service, to boost up my neighbor, my family in grace,
For so short is life, but a breath on earth's face, and judgment I sift for the worth of this race.

New Day Arising

We know not what sorrow shall blossom this day,
Nor torment beset us like demons at play.
Our hopes lay resolved to endure endlessly
This warped, sin-sick world, all dark evil to flee.

This life and death struggle we wage to the end,
Though faith in the Champion shall victory send.
No flesh can disarm us, the triumph assured;
As strife-proven soldiers we live by His word.

Austria. *Sometimes the battles men face are literal, and involve head-to-head clashes with the enemy. We cannot back up, but must face these battles squarely, and hope that our spouses and children will not be left without us once the smoke and haze clear after the fight.*

Fight On in This Race of Life

No Fear to Flee

How kind a God, and good, to thrust my feet into the fire of earthly conflict continually,
That I might learn to trust in Him forever, each moment,
And face these fears — these uncouth unpleasantries — and conquer this flight from pain,
To overcome this wicked culture implanted by the Adversary, the friend of disease and disorder,
So I may face these challenges and foes thrown at me to test and refine …
And yet stand while all else falls around me.

Onward

Broken of spirit, bowed down in pain of life, agonies of living, rejection by men,

    I move yet forward,
    The only road open,
    For the road behind leads death-ward.

Pathways of life escape me, though the one upon which I tread is the only course open,

    So I walk upon it,
    Throwing caution to the wind,
    Flinging selfish emotion aside. *Continued on page 26*

Alaska. *A caribou in the northern climes of Alaska must forage diligently throughout the summer to store up enough energy to endure the bitter cold of winter. So must we as sojourners on the earth eat of the truth daily and store up the spiritual provender that will carry us through the many battles we fight.*

Fight On in This Race of Life

Continued from page 25

So often darkness obscures the way, but lights beyond forever
enlighten my sight

To view beyond the present,
To crave future brilliance …
So present pain is thrust away.

No matter the flesh, though care for it well, but unveil the spirit,

And grasp the reins
Of thundering white horses
Plunging down upon Babylon's realm.

Passion

Live today, though dreams elude you,
With fervent play amid your days few.

Porter, Minnesota. *The peace of a cool, fresh river of living water
always greets the weary warrior in the battle to overcome in this
highly imperfect world, one beset by many barriers during the
race along the strait and narrow pathway.*

Fight On in This Race of Life

The Fight Goes On

The fight I fight never ends.
It pursues me to the far corners of the earth,
Testing my foundation as a hurricane buffets
A house anchored upon the Rock.
My shortcomings ever pursue me
As agonizing, brutal enemies
Prepared to attack in times of weakness …
Which are many.
But I fight the good fight,
Even when weak and unable to carry on,
Even when tormented at death's very door.
I must carry on with hope unending,
Joy abounding through this suffering temple
For a little while … yes, just a little while.

The Race of Life

Each morning, sun arising — a fiery ball —
My body longs for motion, sinews cry for action,
And once again legs ply the well-trodden road,
The secret paths through field and forest
Known only to this wayfaring soul.

Life's microcosm replayed each new day, I test the waters:
Wind at my back, so easily the miles slip by
Amongst rocks, swaying brown grass, and windblown oaks …
Or wind in my face, cold and fierce, tears streaming,
Lungs aching and tired legs churning, crying to keep the pace.

Continued on page 29

Fight On in This Race of Life

Continued from page 28

I move on, always move on, seldom resting,
For the good man cannot imagine giving up,
Or even slowing amidst the challenges of wind, icy paths,
Rocky precipices, or the black wall of failings …
Such thoughts never entering spirit-filled dreams.

So I press on against the tests, not fearing the pain,
Rejoicing in this trial I know must be faced again and again
To harden the muscles, to melt the armor of fear,
To strengthen my heart amongst the hills and vales of life's antipathy,
And run the race of restless life once again.

Work On!

Though hopes be dim for days' endeavors thick,
Amidst the pains of efforts tough and quick,
I set my gaze on lights beyond the gloom,
And pray that sweat exerted shall exhume
The grief of sinful masters whose instruction
Has in past years wreaked such grim destruction.
So as for me the course reads proverbs sage:
The righteous man works on though darkness rage.

Mission

What is life, that I should be
A forlorn creature on the sea
Of roiling, foaming, soulless night,
Abiding trials where few delight.

Yet on I must forge through the foam;
There is no other course to home,
That gleaming City where the pain
I feel today is crushed and slain.

This life I hear so often groan
Is but a visage of my own
Eternal wisdom's far-flung calls,
"Return to former splendor's halls."

As long as breath remains within
This supple flesh abhorring sin,
Then ever will this blinded world
Reject my freedom oft unfurled.

Seldom noted do I sit,
A lone crusader, candle lit
To guide the forlorn down the path
That winds where crystal waters laugh.

Saints Forgotten

Those who are termed great in this world
May be remembered in name through centuries,
Though their personage be forgotten …
But countless saints are never remembered,
Though inheritors of eternal abodes
Far beyond the fading pride of flesh …
Their spotless lives never to be forgotten.

Russia. *So many people put their trust in the kings and princes of the world's governments, thinking they will bring security and happiness, but these leaders are usually self-centered and blind to spiritual truths, glorifying short-term gain. Our future life depends on our knowledge and obedience to the truths that are eternal.*

Chapter 6 Future Life

The Future

My heart can never allow to slumber
This soul yet unfulfilled,
When quickly slip the years by number —
Lost time, her wages skilled.

I look behind … what roads were built
Amongst the fearsome storms,
My ship beset by pain and guilt,
Will bent for life reform.

To what, I ask, shall this deep mystery
Seek to make life worthy,
For half its mission lies in history,
The other half before me.

Life should be simple, speaks the wizard
Of my childhood daydreams,
But seasoned through the howling blizzard
I know tomorrow's course-streams …

Shall mold this soldier's future age
In ways he never dreams;
Former paths were to presage
The future's awesome schemes …

And I cannot sit still
Until my last breath has fathomed the Eternal's will.

Farmington, New Mexico. *What is it about towering, solitary mountains that so intrigues the human heart? Is it the embedded memory from millennia past that reminds us of the mountain of God, the heavenly Zion that is the residence of the very Creator who made us and all things in the world, and is the future residence of the elect from which they will come down and reign on the earth?*

Chapter 7

Guarding the Mind

Compromise

There is no end to compromising Truth 'midst seas of stormy tales,
For when the first dissenting cries are heard within our conscience fair,
And we in lemming-like procession fail to thwart the angry swales
Soon discover dikes are breached, and floods o'er-flow perfection's lair.

Hiding

The truest test of character is what you do alone,
Hidden from accusing faces, peering judges' eyes;
Thence proceeds the real persona, stripped of flesh and bone,
Motivations clear, unfettered from false image lies.

When actions wrong convict the soul, one's righteousness corrupt,
All systems surge to guard that image conscience has constructed …
Unite soul, mind, and body, vain destruction interrupt,
Reality of God's omniscient vision be instructed.

Portals of the Mind

Guard carefully the portals of your mind,
For what enters remains
To please and edify, or taunt and degrade,
And lasts days and weeks in either case,
Which sometimes years cannot erase,
Reminding the consciousness of good or evil.
May the good enter and reign!
Guard carefully the portals of your mind.

Colombia.

Like a precious ancient gold vessel of incalculable worth, so is the mind in its intricate design and function, capable of performing tasks many times more complicated and innovative than the most sophisticated computers ever built. What goes into that mind must be guarded at all costs.

When Guilt Is Gone

While ocean swells pound mightily upon my sea of contentment,
And grief spurns fair passions while this act is played out,
Is not guilt and one's freedom from its clutches an eternal destiny,
To be harbored safely from the rising swells
While pondering future hopes and dreams … the real substance of life?

So warm life proceeds forth in fashion each day,
Each heartfelt creation, each passion and sway,
While absurd repugnance of festering guilt,
Remains safely hidden, a crown rarely built.
For short life's bid pathways remain straiter now,
And strait and narrow to lead the ship's prow
Through seas calm or boiling, but never at rest
Until firmly seated by love's last request.

Continued on page 37

Continued from page 36

Thrust out guilt's dark pain and its stifling grip,
For from perfect love and compassion one sips
The death knell of bondage that past held its sway,
Before understanding of life knew its way.
Without fear of man's ways, but of God, what sits
Astride the black monster that evil plot knits,
While honor, truth, patience, humility, joy,
Remembrance of mercy, forgiveness deploy …

The antithesis of this world and its selfish ways,
Which thrust great burdens upon unsuspecting and well-meaning mankind,
Whose hopes lie festering, dashed finally to bits amid the shambles of empires past,
When men's hopes gasped for truth, to be dampened yet a bit longer.

Oh, sheepish fools of man's fate, thrust out the guilt you yet harbor,
And shine forth the mystery of Eden for all to grasp.
Recall that guilt is past,
    removed far from the malingering clutches of your shattered mind-threads,
Whose past is future, whose threads descend from on high,
    whose nostalgia remains but as memories …

While a better world awaits,
Beyond sequestered gates;
On earth in patience lies,
Its hopeful teacher's eyes,
In search of cities fair,
Ambassadors to share
A kingdom not yet hence …
Return to peace and sense.

New Zealand. *Like the relentless pounding of sea waves upon rocks, so guilt can mercilessly pound away upon our conscience, threatening to dislodge our sense of worth and accomplishment. The removal of guilt — to realize one's incredible worth and cast away every burden that impedes our journey — is the beginning of life abundant as living is intended.*

Heroism

Chapter 9

True Heroism

There thrives a certain heroism,
    fraught among men of skillful soul,
Who fear not fierce storms,
    even death's clutches amidst the enclosing darkness.
They thrive on stresses strong,
    adversities which set their resolve ever so keenly,
Trials laughed at, the price of victory not weighed,
    the portent of greater dreams
Sought fervently while pressing forward
    through the forbidding fog of night.

Black Hills, South Dakota. *There are many so-called heroes for every nation, those that risked their lives to cement a new constitution for a new people. Yet, there are heroes in everyday living who are not noted in history books and are forgotten, but may have done more for the betterment of mankind than those we laud in books or on mountains.*

Chapter 10

Hope

Progress

I hasten down the long and dusty road,
In search of footprints where a Friend has strode.
My eyes are quick to spot the telltale signs
Which joyously grow plainer with each time
The farthest hill now rests beneath my feet,
And yonder hill seems possible to reach.

Alaska. *A rainbow symbolizes the promise that the earth will never again be destroyed by water, but it also displays light separated into its respective colors that give brilliance and variety to all things on earth, colors that animate life and grant hope in our daily living.*

Idols

An idol — so small a word, so seemingly simple a thought —
Yet incorrigibly comprehensive in its devastation,
Insidiously corrupting in its subtle schemes.
We know not its toll until in tears our hearts crumble.

An idol, that object of adoration set above heaven,
Shines forth its message of obedience,
Encompassing fond hopes and dreams of the unwary,
Commanding the foolish serve anything but their Maker.

British Columbia, Canada. *Idols abound in our world, not just the carved images of native American tribes and Pacific Islanders, in which people believed that spirits actually inhabited these inanimate objects, but they have flourished throughout all nations in the things people place before their Creator, from houses to automobiles to ranches and coin collections.*

Chapter 12

Judgement

Logs

As time flees by I step along the meandering footpaths of forests,
Noting the glaring sores that stain the logs long crashed to earth.
My friend, despise not those unsightly stains so quickly noted,
Those sores of imperfection, staining excellent repute ...
For your own logs so often disrupt your clear view
Of the innocent of heart whose fidelity exceeds your own,
And whose passion for good might alarm your presumptuous imagination .

Utah. *An upright, beautiful tree can fall and decay into a twisted remnant of its original self, much like any of us who might falsely accuse someone of an error he may have committed ... but which your own sins far exceed.*

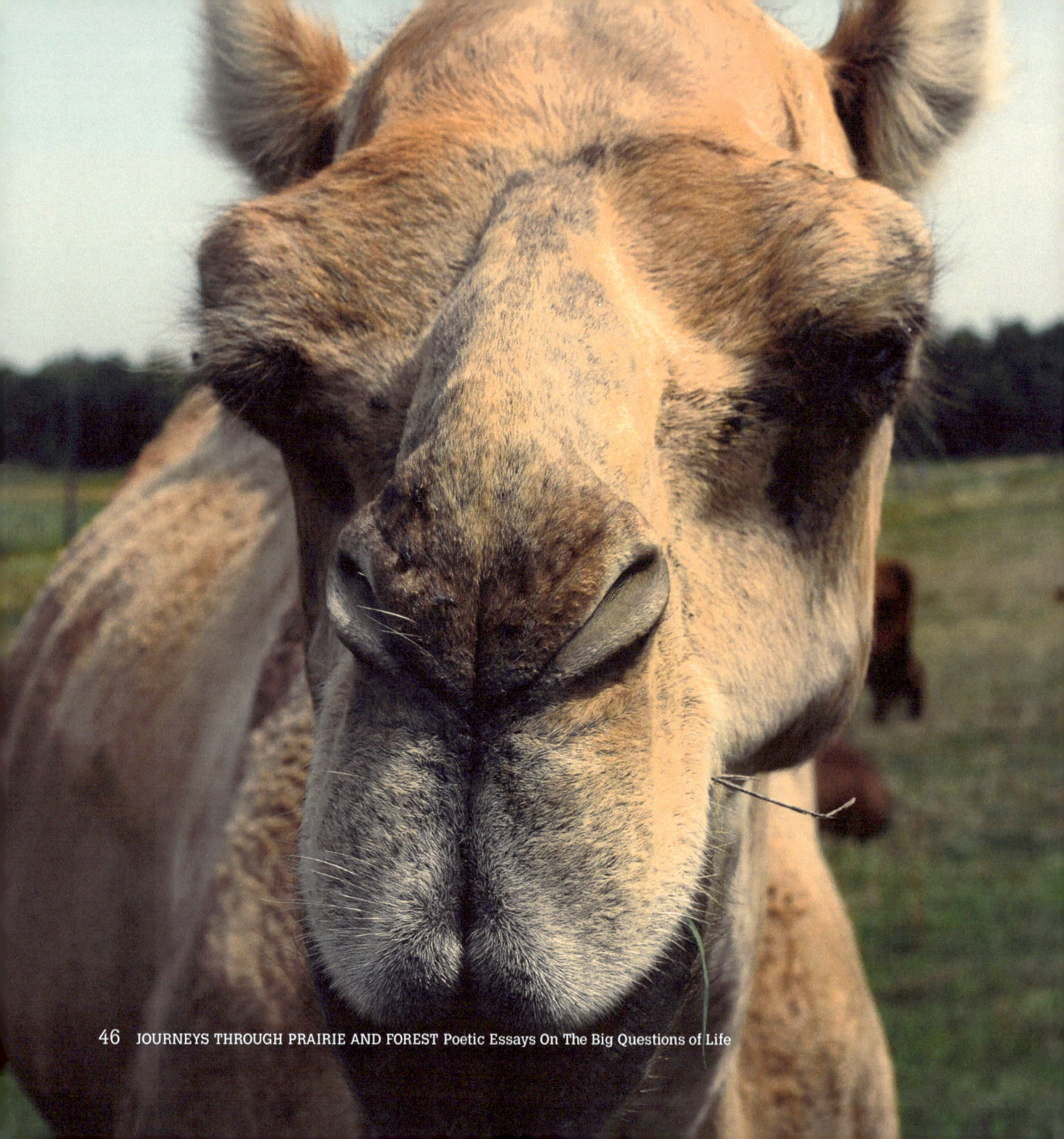

JOURNEYS THROUGH PRAIRIE AND FOREST Poetic Essays On The Big Questions of Life

Know Yourself

Acceptance

Accept the being that God has made of you,
Flesh and blood ordered in His very image
To be nourished in the spirit of power and love,
Demolishing erroneous views of self, Satan's accusations
Hurled from the stormy depths of his perversion,
Seeking to belittle the ones the Creator has made,
Thrusting fiery darts towards their worth,
Denying their eternal heritage in wanton imagination,
While awesome foreverness sings within the breasts
Of those forever sealed among heaven's fiery stones.

Attics

With deep, upwelling excitement and anticipation I ascend the dusty attic stairway,
Peering this way and that amongst musty books, boxes, and clothes,
Seeking something … of ages past, other folks' lives, truths dangling here and there
So I might secretly understand myself better, see my inner being …
That daily voyage through inner space I intensely partake of
In suffering and fear, that tomorrow may bring great consolation,
Hopes and dreams within this child of clay, a bit better known to myself,
Even as I am known.

South Dakota. *Self-identity is so critical for living each day to the fullest. Even an inquisitive animal living far outside of its normal habitat can know its own nature and thrive in spite of the strange surroundings.*

Know Yourself

Be Yourself

Be yourself, no one else, one whom God has formed,
In His image, fruitful visage of His awesome Being;
Shining face, as brass your breast, a rainbow o'er your throne
Here on earth, no less a son of God than the Firstborn.

Horseshoes

I labored valiantly to fill the role
Carved out through millennia of sweat and tears
That moulded my father, his father, and fathers for generations before,
While all the while I pitied the lost self.

Then I reached down … just a little ways —
And picked up a horseshoe … it wasn't very heavy —
And pitched it in the usual manner toward the stake,
A mere forty feet distant.

The manner I tried to emulate in this throw
Derived itself from the world champion I had seen — no less —
Whose shoes seldom missed, so deftly they flew,
That their resounding strike home each throw left little to imagine.

My shoes would bob and weave; oh, they struck home now and then,
But frustrated this arm would swing
On past my knee as the pro-man did.
Yet, mine would sink when his would rise, and bob or wave while his would not.

Continued on page 51

Rocky Mountain National Park, Colorado.
The peace and solitude of a cold, pristine mountain lake is the perfect place to look inward at the self and acknowledge more perfectly the person that you are.

Sinai, South Dakota. *Few sports are more challenging to the soul than horseshoe pitching. Any slight deviance from the prescribed throw will send the shoe on an erroneous course that will miss the mark, requiring the thrower to continually monitor his style and know his weakness to prevent too many errors.*

Continued from page 48

Then in disgust — in vile torment —
I threw the wretched theory aside
Of emulating in every detail the champion,
But pulled my wits together and said,

"Let's see a bit of ME!"

So I did. I threw them on, straight on;
Oh, not quite so well as the pro-man, but quite well I must say …
For on went one, another, and another,
    striking home despite the gathering darkness of night …
A handsome six of ten — not bad, not bad.

May not this thick head perceive the lesson
Of steel upon steel, precept upon precept?
Where was the germ which carved this mind,
This body fitly tied …

To which I reply,
"Who am I to decide?"

I'm Still Me

The days roll by, full of stardom or obscurity.
Ages continue unabated despite my bluster or humility,
And tears are shed behind my back, as if my own eyes were cheating.
Despots rise and fall, empires swell mightily, yet only to tumble.

Harmony decays into rancour and disarray, only to discover itself once more from the rabble.
On and on march the ages, mankind choosing his own futile paths.

And all through the blindness of man's vain choices,
I'm still me. *Continued on page 52*

Chapter 13 Know Yourself

Continued from page 51

The day's voice rings forth as an operatic composure across the frozen plains of time,
While ancient minds ponder the reasons for living, but find nothing that is new,
    sublime, or worthy.
A thousand Napoleans, ten thousand Rembrandts, a million Voltaires, a score of Einsteins,
    or myriads in Aristotle's image flash brilliantly across the stage, only with much less
    décor and imagination, more drab and serene, more homely and less pompous ... yet
    there they were in their glory which time and chance failed to reveal,

        And as they were, as all of them were,
        I'm still me.

Countless struggles beset my soul,
Of days gone by — yes — the memories linger,
When status lay amid heaps of jewels, gold, and estates,
Humanity's most imperial virtues lying dormant, untouched, as pure as prime vintage,
    but unnoticed.
Strive as one may to lay claim to the genius of others — their styles, gifts, faculties,
    individuality — they elude hungry grasps, and thankfully so ...
For theirs is their own, and greed knows no bounds.
As ranting and raving rise vehemently amid a troubled sea,
What folly lies blatantly seen, a log in the eye so transparent it seems.

        So you're still you and ...
        I'm still me.

Try to alter the self, what the Creator has deftly made, and what remorse one meets,
When inborn behaviors become sorted from captured skills.
The vile, demented acquired mind-patterns indeed must depart,
But inherent skills retained to grow and blossom as roses upon a bland and faceless plain.

Continued on page 53

Know Yourself

Continued from page 52

So the mind sees itself and cringes, and commences its change, like a ship cast out to sea,
   rudder firmly in hand, with a billion shipmates in their own boats roiling the sea about,
   yet themselves unable to upset your own.
The sea is treacherous, yet the ship undauntable, unsinkable, impervious to the pounding waves
   about it that threaten to dilute the cultured gray matter in the hold.

   So though waves break over my head,
   I'm still me.

A hundred seabirds fly overhead in the pristine clear blue sky,
Heralding land but a short distance away.
The view heavenward is clear, but a mist shrouds my view of the sea and the shore,
Where lives linger among their daily tasks, completed briskly and with purpose,
Seeking prosperity and worthwhile gain — yet beyond my grasp and reason … only in a dream.
The mist begins to clear, revealing azure vistas of truth, hope, worthwhile endeavor,
   where before was striving after the wind,
A fierce wind that deflated both heart and soul.

   And as truth clears the skies, I look, and …
   I'm still me.

I always have been, but had not looked in the mirror.
Yet, had I looked before the proper time my mind could not have drunk in the revolting sight.
How often is insight into the self so frightening, to expose in its own murky truth?
Yet, come fame or less, come hope or distress, come plenty or famine, or truth or love saddened,
I need never fear, through days or nights here,
Or in other worlds, beyond this realm's pearls,

Through light or dark, ups or downs,
Good or evil, it doesn't really matter what one meets on life's pathways, for whatever the case,
   and whatever the cause,
   I'm still me,
   And always will be.

Know Yourself

Know Yourself

Strive to know yourself,
And be not afraid of who you are,
For God has made you as He willed —
At this time, at this place —
For a great purpose which in time shall be revealed.
Be not ashamed for your personage,
Made in God's image for infinitely good works and honor,
That in the fullness of time shall be revealed
To the glory and uplift of all creation!

Austria.
People who have changed the course of history — for good or for evil — are lauded in history books and the media, but each person made in the image of Elohim is of just as great value, but is never given the exposure of stardom or fame in this world.

Know Yourself

Learning to Be

Tried by flames, often singed by fire,
This soul of light treads forests dark and dire,
Delivered from the blinding feral prison
Of long-lost hopes and unrepentant vision.

We must know who we are … and so we know
That aging bodies may restore the flow
Of fathers' wisdom sighing deep within,
Plumes of passion dashing sin's last hymn.

How can our meager selves the trials bear
Success in overcoming grievous snares,
The self in sullen madness standing fast,
Refusing change of habits life has cast?

Oh, self-made will, how can you reach the fame
Our great Creator cast within your name?
The genes, the cells, now code your new-found place,
A seat amongst the Master's firstfruits race!

Sinai, South Dakota. *All around us are found the incomparable beauty and fragrance of the creation, especially amongst the flowers with their infinite variety, all pointing to the awesome character of the One who made them, and in whose image people are made. Getting to know that One is the first step in knowing the self.*

Chapter 14

Marginalized

Pushed to the Margins

The heart aches deep within, through separation from spirit kin,
Thrust away with man's concocted dreams, of Caesar's courts approving ill-led schemes,
Which etch the heart with stone, its tenderness to hades thrown,
And those whose wisdom differs get thrown to dungeons bitter,
Pushed to margins — mind and space — well beyond one's proper place.
And thus I sit in bondage thrice, with Galileo, Tesla, and Semmelweis,
So suffer house arrest and pain, pushed to margins 'cross this plain,
Clinging mightily to truth, while Pharisees throw darts uncouth.

> My place in this world's scheme I deem
> Is in Christ's footsteps and His ageless dream.

Removed to the Margins

We sit awestruck, yet serenely, on the margins of this world's culture,
Surrounded by seas of tumult, yet closing our ears to the din, so muffled and distant,
Turning away from the dour ugliness of man's society constructed of wood and idols,
A seething fleshpot of sin and corruption … yet out of reach to those not partaking,
Lost in time's misadventure, sitting on the edge …

My slave girl and myself,
Purchased from captivity in Egypt;
We have together crossed the Red Sea,
And the Promised Land is oh so near,
Oh, so very real …

> But only because we sit at the margins of man's culture,
> His lost throes of misguided adventure heaping insult upon insult

Continued on page 59

Egypt. *The Israelites were led out of Egypt by Moses through a forbidding desert to the shores of the Red Sea, after being forced by the Eternal through a series of devastating plagues to let them go. So often we are likewise pushed to the margins of society by unfriendly forces despite doing good, and are led through the wilderness of this culture into a better land.*

Continued from page 58

Upon true destiny, proper environment, lawful living,
Thrust out of Eden to survive through war, suffering, disease, death …
Mirth long forgotten, true joy fleeing — not comprehended —
Amidst Egypt's fleshpots, the great morass of life's sea boiling in discontent.
And we are thrust to the margins, far from the center,
That giant whirlpool of corrupt values so repulsive to the enlightened.

We sit, we cry for lost souls dragged towards the center of the vortex,
Ceaselessly swirling towards oblivion in the steaming morass …
Secure and peaceful amidst insanity and discontent,
On the margins, unable to latch on to those rejecting the outstretched hand,
Shunned by throngs, friends of few,
But always ready, always waiting …
For the edge to become the center.

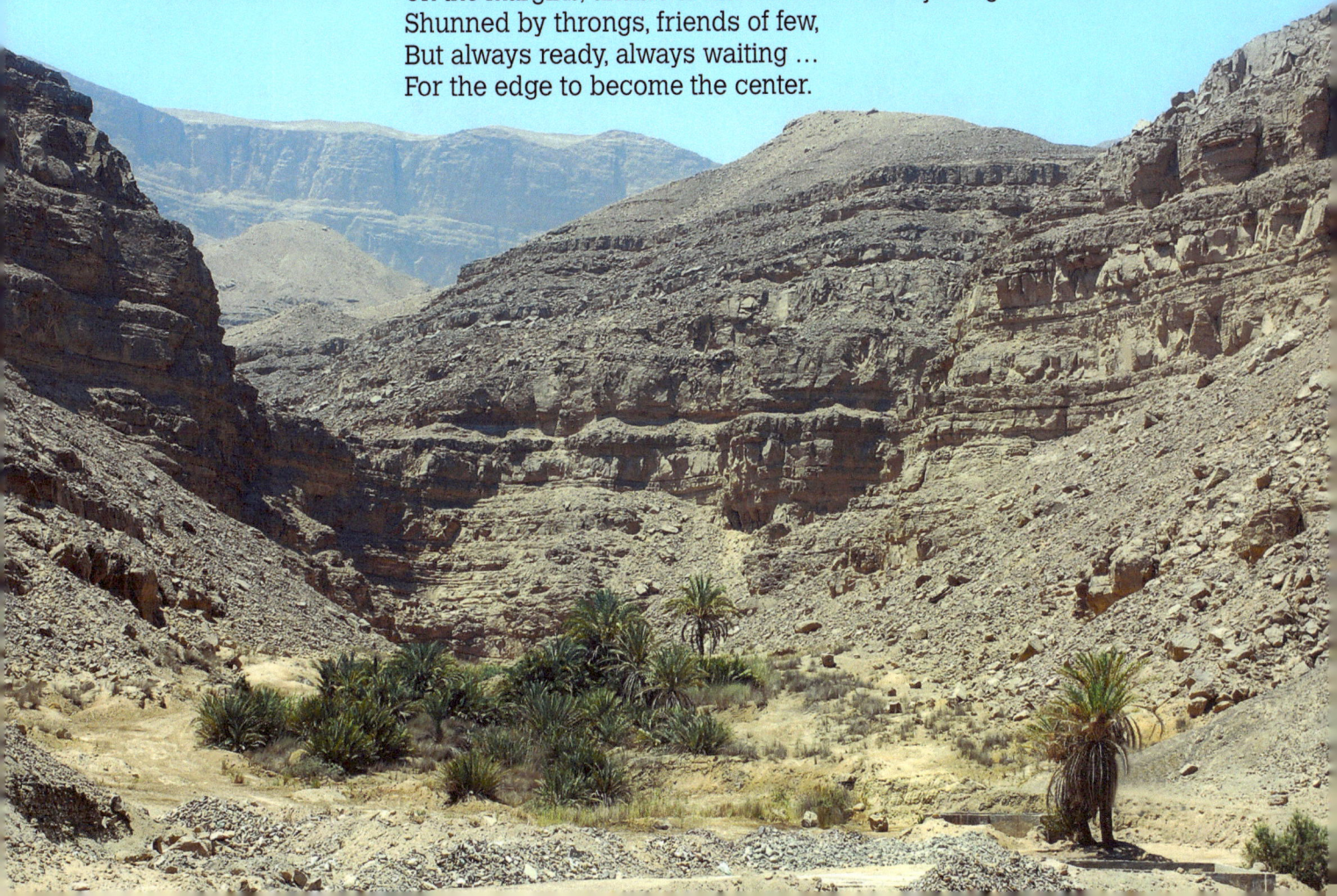

Egypt. *As gigantic sentinels upon the plain overlooking Cairo, Egypt, so the pyramids remind us to aspire to the challenges we face daily in life and figuratively, in our personal lives, climb to the pinnacles of these awesome relics of an ancient civilization.*

Overcoming

Chapter 15

Forget Not …

We must not forget the trialsome times that forged our lives today,
The pains and sufferings we endured for a season, so easily forgotten,
So instructive for our present state, givers of direction in times past
That tomorrow's perils may be endured and overcome with wisdom.

Generations Relived

Each new child, every being, spirit template of earth's dreaming,
Must of needs learn all anew, each his lesson, dreams a'scheming,
Of truth that reigns through ages past, future that shall ever last;
So all seek their Maker's face, assured of His praiseworthy cast.

Agreed I not to grace the earth — its teeming sin, this witch's brew —
In this dark age where thrust into the maelstrom we of flesh must view
Embarrassments unending placed before us which our fathers fought;
So likewise we endure the cost, regain the victories they lost.

Onward speed these shortened days, I know not where they flee,
Yet confident I stand that pathways granted shall agree
With He who molded this brief moment for His glorious nation,
Generations lost from view revived in exaltation.

Lost Souls

Lost souls cast upon the waters of discontent,
Not knowing their course, nor destinations far flung,
Across the roiling waters, watched solemnly by fiery serpents;
Forlorn hearts searching desperately like off-cast floating islands,
For foundations to anchor hope, to cease drifting,
To gain footing on far-off sacred shores.

A Message to Lost Souls

In bondage lost souls sink
Beneath the rushing waters of culture's slavery,
Like cold and lifeless stones,
Reliving the history of paradise lost.

Out from this chaotic depth of captivity
Must lost souls break free and swim upwards
From captivity to the perfect light above,
That life may begin anew.

Melancholy

Melancholy, lethargy, lack of productivity,
Mind in clouds of stray mind-bits,
Searching for life's tender wits
That turn the fray towards victory,
Destroying vain captivity.

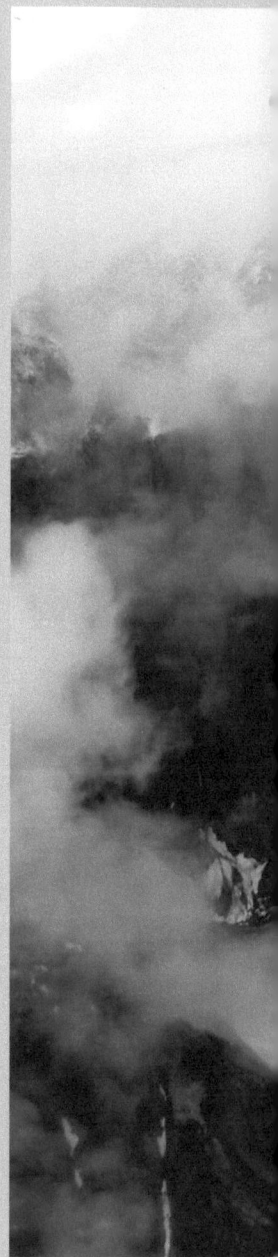

Denali National Park, Alaska.
Glacial ice flows slowly through the huge valleys between mountain peaks, carrying along anything in their way. So must we with relentless persistence overcome the stubborn trials we face on a daily basis, remembering we are not alone in this breathtaking adventure.

Persistence and Endurance

Never Give Up

Never give up the fight, for victory is at hand.
Never remove your gaze from the goal, for He shall sustain you.
Forsake not the calling your Maker has given you, for its fruits are everlasting.
Continue on in earnest, knowing your fiery trial shall not continue forever,
And your change shall build sanctuaries of perfection upon foundations of gold.

Awaiting Deliverance

Late summer's pungent, acrid air,
Steeped with new-fallen rain, a bit to lighten drought's bitterness,
Wafts lazily beneath starlight's shrouded vista,
Darkness resting uneasily within these straits of hope …
A family pensively awaiting deliverance from Egypt's captivity,
To release the bonds of debt and predation.

> Oh, slavery, where lies your sting?
> When shall your estate fade away?

Morning's light shall bring new fields of waving grain,
Billowing clouds amongst the chambers of Zion,
Singing birds, grazing kine, bubbling brooks …
Not just imagined while waiting helplessly in dreams,
But the solidity of true deliverance,
From whence this dreamy waiting shall burst forth
Into life abundant once again!

Badlands National Park, South Dakota. *Water eroding sedimentary strata year in and year out over centuries can create remarkable features in multi-colored rocks, revealing how patient action can reveal wonderful results if we simply persist.*

Persistence and Endurance

Holding Firm

This captive world holds man and beast
To desperation, toil and grief ...
Sheer survival ever thrust
To testing 'midst the mire and dust.

     Yet ...

Here I stand despite the storm,
Holding firm the altar's horn;
Though tossed upon earth's roiling sea
I cast my will to God's decree.

In His Hands

All the works of men are in Your hands.
The earth and its wonders of field and forest, mountain and plain, are filled with Your wisdom,
Each beautiful green leaf crying forth Your great righteousness and creative strength.
The deliciously fragrant north breeze carries with it clear understanding of Your kindness,
Kind and magnificent as the purifying sunlight beaming forth from above, caressing hilltop
and valley with life in abundance.
The very works of men and their civilizations throughout history are in Your grasp,
For You harden hearts and You loosen them, You lift up kings and nations and depose them.
All things are in Your hands, great God, and I marvel at Your wonderful truth which cannot be
hidden from the seeking heart.
Open wide the doors of Your truth, Almighty One, and pour forth Your abundant wisdom,
knowledge, and understanding into this searching mind.
Prepare my being for the things that are to come, and release me from the grip of fear that
threatens to steal away the crown You have reserved for me.

China. *Over a period of about 2,000 years a wall of over 6,000 miles was built across northern China to try and keep out the Mongolian hordes. Persistent effort through many dynasties was required to complete this gigantic task, which brought relative safety for millions of Chinese.*

JOURNEYS THROUGH PRAIRIE AND FOREST Poetic Essays On The Big Questions of Life

Persistence and Endurance

Keep Going

Stride bravely toward the light 'midst thorns and painful test;
Though blood may blur your sight, cease not the weary quest,

For not far down the lane of life your hopes will never fade,
Joy's victory midst the pain, bold sacrifice repaid.

Forge On!

Never give up the fight, for victory is at hand.
Never remove your gaze from the Goal, for He shall sustain you.
Forsake not the calling your Maker has given you, for its fruits are everlasting.
Forge ahead in earnest, knowing your fiery trial shall not continue forever,
And your change shall build sanctuaries of perfection upon foundations of gold.

Move Ever Forward

The cry at midnight resounds, "Move on, do not turn back, never give up the battle!"
So I turn not aside to escape the terrible battle looming on ahead,
    the horrible strife relegated to the hopeful in heart …
As my heart sinks and slides through manifold temptations,
    while the Adversary hurls his fiery darts
To dissuade the strongest hearts from brilliant victory amidst the deep and darkened night.

Continued on page 70

France. *Complete with flying buttresses and immaculate stonework, Notre Dame cathedral took 200 years to complete during the Gothic period, an example of what mankind can do when applying superb engineering skills along with persistent effort … a lesson for each of us in our own skill of choice.*

chapter 16

Persistence and Endurance

Continued on page 69

"Move on, lead on towards the victory!",
    so my weary body cries though the fray,
Never turning back, not relenting in spite of weakness and depravity
Of flesh so wrinkled, of mind so humbled.

"Lead on, come forward young soul!"
And onward I strive indeed,
Words of men lacking clarity to speak eternal wisdom,
But resting upon that bulwark ever loyal
To comfort His chosen ones,
And grant them the victory above the strongest enemies.

The Reward of Persistence

Never cease the quest for life!
Then all of your paths shall be mightily established.
Your children and grandchildren shall flourish and overspread the earth,
And your legacy of faithfulness and love will never be snuffed out,
But continue forever shining through the darkness of eons past,
    and those to come …
For the Eternal knows no bounds, nor does time limit His exploits.
Praise the One who brings down, but in pity raises up,
That you might soar like eagles
And never, never be ashamed to live!

Colombia. *Though the field may be large and the tools small, yet the persistent hoeing of only a few dedicated farmers can complete the task as they pursue their work one minute at a time, enduring the summer heat until the job is done.*

Persistence and Endurance

Not My Will …

My soul cried for food:

   It was given the Bread of Life.

My heart longed for friends:

   It was granted brethren.

My mind craved knowledge of all things:

   It was given wisdom of higher things.

My spirit sought release from loneliness:

   It found kinship with those seeking my friendship.

My being sought a permanent resting place:

   It received a mansion reserved in Zion.

My desire was to leave this world of pain and suffering:

   It was told to wait for the regeneration of times.

My God would not let me leave this tabernacle just yet,

   For I must patiently wait yet a little longer … a little longer.

Bryce Canyon National Park, Utah. *How the vertical outcrops of a canyon can form through persistent water erosion cannot be envisioned by a person in his short lifetime, but the example of persistent effort is openly displayed for all of us to see and emulate.*

Persistence and Endurance

Our Fierce Battle

We, the faithful, can never rest in this life,
For conflict ever besets us, our battle with the unseen powers,
Never at peace with the Adversary's fiery darts ever around us.
We clutch the Master's hand and step forth bravely into the black of night,
Ever hopeful that tomorrow will bring us respite from this daily fight,
The battle ever so fierce and pivotal that all creation depends on our success,
A world that waits in hushed expectancy for our victory.

Reflections On a Melancholic Eve

I know not tomorrow's harvest of exploits,
Nor the measure of today's hard-fought battles
That threaten the fortress of my hope and stability,
Thrusting through my bubble of self-virtue with the sword,
Making a mockery of this soul's well-manicured image.

Oh, show me friends when none seem true.
Grant me ample provision to fill that great hunger
Which lay within the bosom of the very elect,
Whose inward parts cry out for compassion amid the fiery trials
Thrown at us without warning.

I cry within as this world's evil spreads its pain
To every creature, to each flower, cloud, and raindrop
Upon my supple face shining heavenward …
The only place I can gaze wherein lies soundness and hope
Amidst the rancor of this cosmos gone mad.

Persistence and Endurance

Seek the Best

So little extra toil it takes to scale the highest heights,
Annihilating commonplace, to reach for stars and lights …
And when the best seems oh-so-far, impossible to reach,
With boundless joy we surge ahead, sublime designs to preach.

Chapter 17

Prayer

Someone Prayed for Me

When first the light began to dawn within my budding soul,
And sin cast forth its ugly head, poured out its lethal bowl,
Revealing just how lost and broken was this shattered life,
And scarcely could all rhyme or reason face the grievous strife,
Then someone prayed for me.

The message sent on high proclaimed in bitterness the pain
To which this soul had slipped and fallen, 'morrow's grievous stain.
There was no hope, it seemed, to come out from the rain,
And all the worthwhile quests in life seemed pointless, toilsome gain.
Then someone prayed for me.

I could not see the pleas go up onto the Father's throne,
But only cry and sigh in darkness, suff'ring all alone.
Then from the depths of night a distant light from heaven shone,
A light that beat the darkness back, to sooth this grievous groan,
For someone had prayed for me.

'Twas not the power of human strength that turned the evil sway,
But some unseen mysterious force that entered me that day.
It turned my life around and saved me 'midst the heated fray,
Because some humble soul took pity on this child of clay,
And prayed for me.

Porter, Minnesota. *A gorgeous sunset signals the end of the day, but can just as easily symbolize the beginning of new life as the colors and patterns envigorate and rejuvenate the soul in need of acquittal from its past.*

18 Predestination

People of All Nations Set in Array

It seems too much a happenstance that men in every nation
Strive to ply their trade in earnest, seeking compensation
For their family's sheer survival in this broken land,
Yet so ordered carefully as by some unseen Hand.

That Hand which whispers to the soul of farmer, mason, doctor,
Go this way, pursue that course, your neighbor needs your offer.
So in the scheme of nation's struggles minds through contemplation,
Might meld forth a hive of intertwined negotiation.

Gentile nation, Israel, the races all reflect
This unseen Hand that orders things … what else could man expect
From His Creator who in wisdom fashioned worlds to dwell,
Hoping men might seek their place in higher worlds as well.

For what more is this life
And its assorted schemes
Than bright reflections of that world
Which yet remains unseen?

Personal Prophesies

Our lives prophetically arranged,
God's children not journeying in vain …
First one country, one state, one village, one field,
Then another and another, across fertile plains to wield
The battle cries of nations cursed,
Their declarations unrehearsed,
Just words put there by God's great mind
To crush the serpent, heal the blind.

Continued on page 81

Guatemala. *A Central American husband treks home with a valuable load of wood on two burros, but how did he arrive in this country in the first place? An unseen hand guided the families of the world to their destinations in a most miraculous way.*

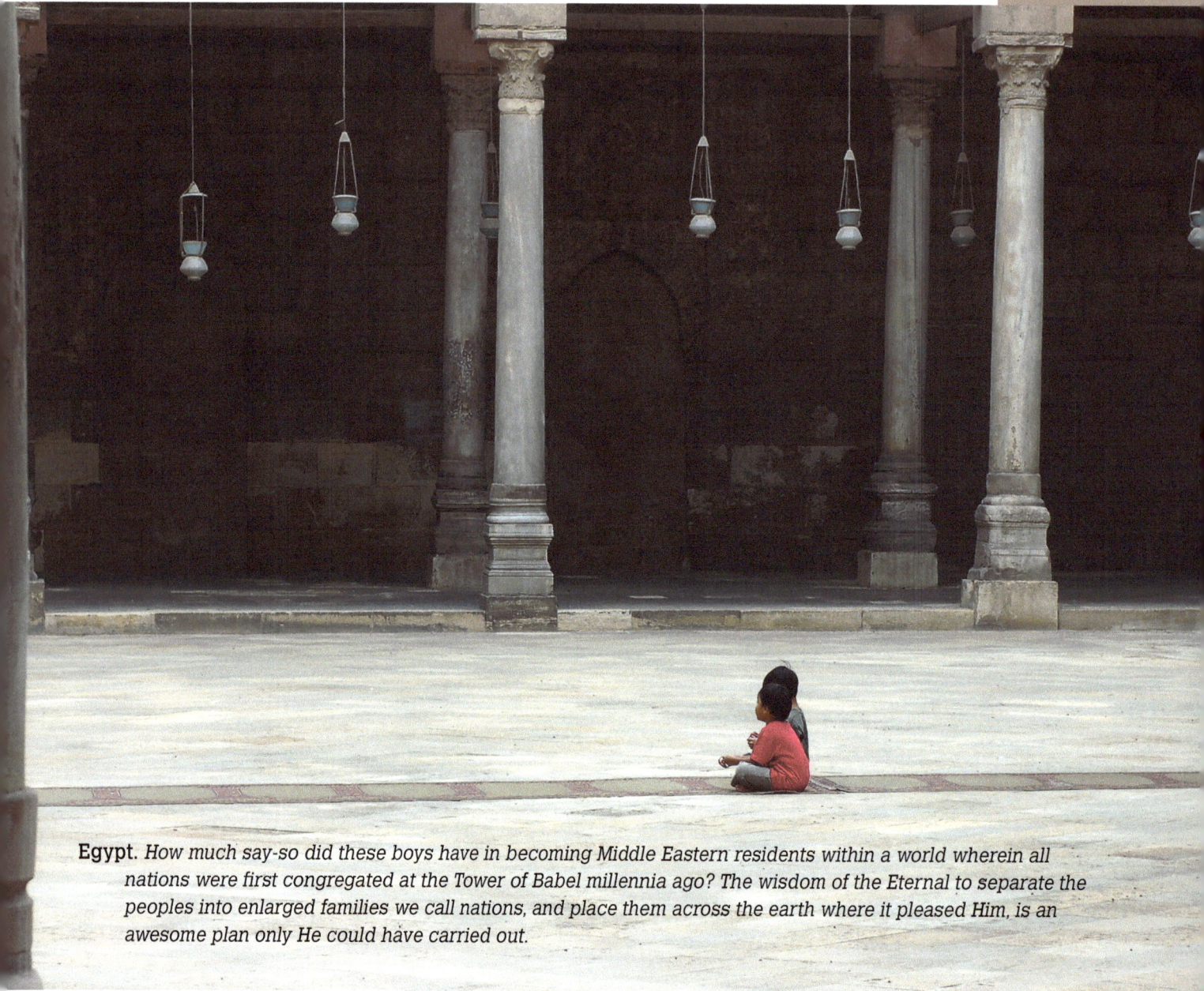

Egypt. *How much say-so did these boys have in becoming Middle Eastern residents within a world wherein all nations were first congregated at the Tower of Babel millennia ago? The wisdom of the Eternal to separate the peoples into enlarged families we call nations, and place them across the earth where it pleased Him, is an awesome plan only He could have carried out.*

chapter 18

Continued from page 78

"Now when the wise men had repaired,
An angel in a dream declared,
'Take the young Child and His mother,
Flee to Egypt lest Herod discover
His whereabouts and kill His soul.'
So Joseph left in haste to go,
Away to Egypt, flee his foe.
But Herod dead, the angel urged,
'Arise and back to Israel surge.'"
So to the town of Nazareth they did flee.
To fulfill the prophesies that a Nazarene He must be.

Though written Scripture won't reveal
The wisdom of the Master's zeal
To each of us, His chosen ones,
With whom He lives beneath His Sun,
Those prophesies in heaven reach
To each of us, His portents teach
That we, as Christ, are just as touched,
Arranged by promises as much,
Revealed in where our lives are healed …
In this poor village, in that lone field.

Predestination

Ordained behavior wields its sway,
Come cloudy storms or sunny day.
Though hard we try to mend our crypt
We actors play out programmed script.

Pride and Vanitiy

Blind Man's Bitter Future

By all appearance to the mortal soul
The culture of this world hath lost its glue,
For dark insanity perfects its role
Amongst a blinded people, not a few.

They mumble through their paces, live the lie
That man his own God is, evolved from slime,
So what can further lie beyond this sky
Than famine's bitter voice, war's evil crime.

Ode to the Overlord

His head up high, voice shouting long
And glorious words of Godly praise,
Pretending that his measured songs
Of timeless precepts would be-daze

A spellbound throng of lowly peasants,
Sitting dutifully and still,
Just to view his awesome presence,
To whom they're taught to bow their will.

Authoritarian zeal unleashed
So squelches free imagination,
Vision's joy — from sin released —
That all His saints might know salvation.

Continued on page 83

Continued from page 82

Yet his lordship, eyes a'glistening,
Harshly orders muted students
To him only should be listening,
"Just obey me!" shouts his instinct.

Yet in humble, meek amazement
Sit the few, the thinking chosen,
Wondering when God's hand in judgment
Should remove false wisdom frozen.

For within God's heavenly diction,
That the greatest is the lowest,
Meek and tired from world's affliction
Future kings in due time flowest.

Now we must maintain our mission
Holding firm to ageless morals,
Singing forth the Law's provision,
Casting out men's darkened laurels.

Moscow. Russia. *The powerful motive to capture the hearts and minds of people by constructing impressive structures is strongly imprinted upon the architecture of church edifices around the world. The elect of God, however, shun such pride, and look towards the things that are humble and of no great earthly reputation.*

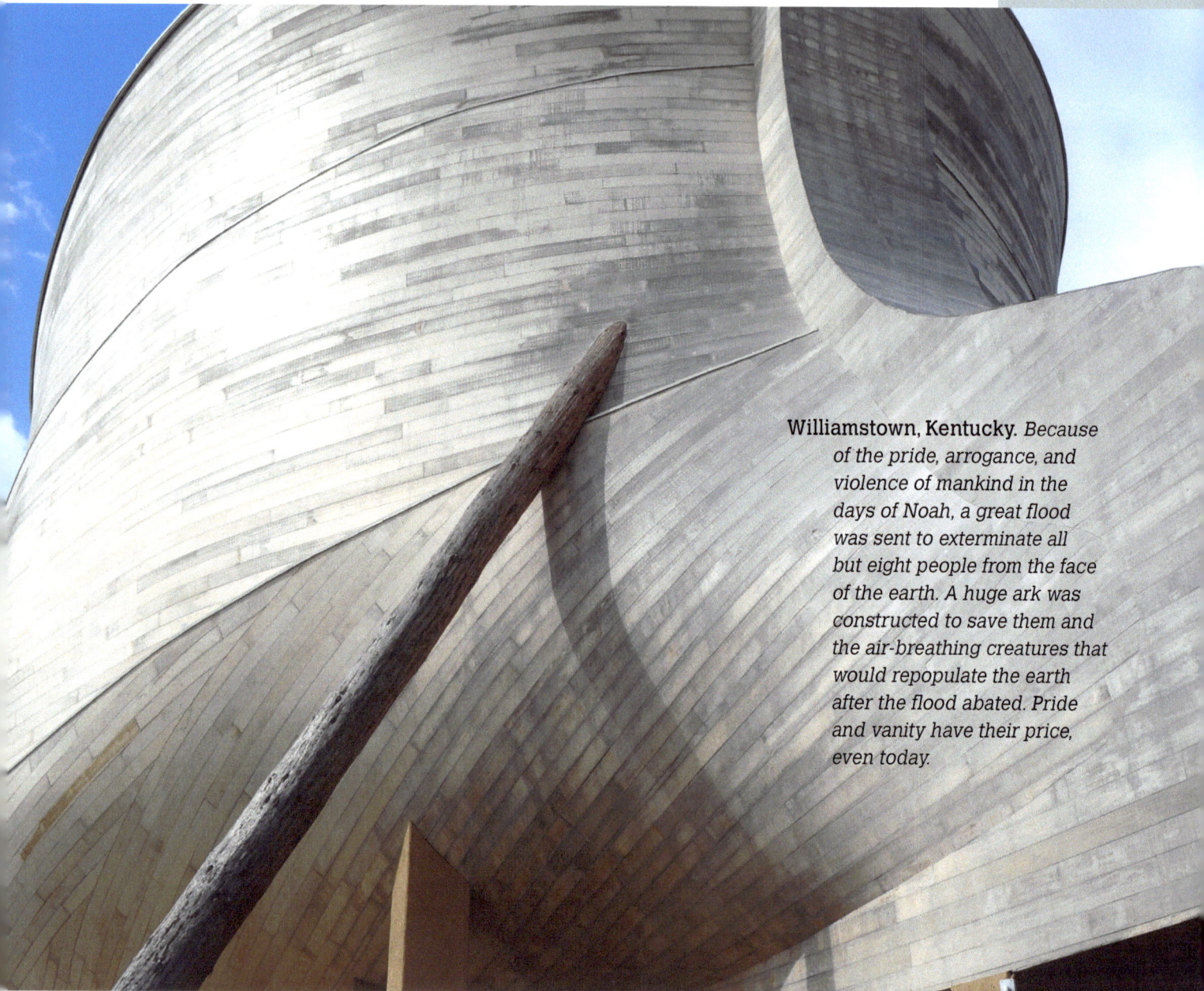

Williamstown, Kentucky. *Because of the pride, arrogance, and violence of mankind in the days of Noah, a great flood was sent to exterminate all but eight people from the face of the earth. A huge ark was constructed to save them and the air-breathing creatures that would repopulate the earth after the flood abated. Pride and vanity have their price, even today.*

Pride and Vanity

The Teacher

He did not strive to be so stern and heavy,
Weighing grievous burdens thick and rapid
Upon the unsuspecting class enrollees,
Grasping for the shouted facts insipid;

But rather felt compelled to hide the mercy
His own home failed to shower on this youngster,
Through countless years a star-struck scholar thirsty
For glory, fame — an ego pricked to bolster.

So on the venom poured through flaming verbiage,
While humbled penmen pounded home instruction,
Searching through the storm for fervent courage,
Untwining erudite and proud deduction.

He could not see the soil a living body,
But rather one large test tube deep and sterile,
Uncouth a bit, though ripe for mankind's study,
So mouths may eat … war's largesse flee from peril.

Few minutes for the unofficial question
Could be enjoyed amidst rapacious hurry,
While slaves enraptured heeded glib instruction
Gesticulated without thought or worry.

It was not meant to be this way, you savvy,
Though soldiers old and grey still understood
That once the seeds of blindness mesh with frenzy
The world itself his space cannot command.

20 Serving Others

Daily Battle

I see the pattern deftly sought, of God's protection ever wrought
Beyond the ranks of mighty warriors, His hands upholding weaker sawyers,
Waging war of gruesome mention … won through holy intervention,
Not by might or ammunition, won by death to self's ambition.

Fearless Leaders

Happy is the man — leader shall he be —
When solidly committed to answering the plea
Of nameless souls bewildered while searching heaven's signs;
He boldly leads — they follow — bright lights of God's designs.

The Needful

It is the proclivity of us warriors
To reach out and search for the one who is lost,
To lift up the sickly one amongst the healthy,
Attend to the needy, those threadbare and naked,
Leaving the 99 and doting upon the one lonely wayfarer
Whose life needs mending, whose coffers are bare.

Guatemala. *The desire to serve others is built into the very inner core of the heart of mankind, unless stifled by experiences and training to squelch this natural desire. Blessed are the families and nations whose leaders are more interested in uplifting others than serving themselves first.*

Sleep Our Teacher

Death we know each night, when in our bed repose
Regains the upper hand, as eyelids softly close.
We know no cause — this death — it simply must return,
Rejuvenating life or sanity we'll spurn.
From life to death, to life again, the cycles flow forsooth,
Bespeaking mysteries unveiled … of resurrection's truth.

Quest for Rest

Live vibrantly yet wisely; cast your cares aside,
Yet knowing many days shall be evil,
And in the end your life will be sacrificed for all men ...
For that is your calling, young man,
And fear not your aging,
Knowing that each day brings you ever closer
To your eternal home,
And rest!

Sleep That Is Me

Sleep, baby, sleep,
Swaddled within cocoons of fantasy in blissful unconsciousness,
Sleeping away in dreams while waking,
Walking among men ... talking among the spirits,
Uncomprehended, uncomprehending ...
The fence is too tall, the cliffs are too high;
Swaddled in innocence, impossible to see clear reality.
Sleep, baby, sleep.
[Of course, that is me.]

Farson, Wyoming.
All creatures need rest, even the birds of the fields and forests. It is essential for living in this age, and a type of the release from servile labor all must experience today, but which the elect will be unburdened from in the coming age.

Sleep Our Healer

Have you afflictions, many a grievous care,
So morning's light brings no joy, life's course in disrepair?
Then feel no guilt should sleep sweep over your soul's lament,
For though poverty shall stalk you with laziness your intent,
Great healing lies within God's bosom, His consolation;
Sleep the sleep of renewal, that world's desolation
Shall not overwhelm your soul of flesh ...
That your spirit He may refresh.

Speaking and Singing

Basic Speech

Communication, communication speakest from the congregation,
Striving hard as one man could, seeking to be understood.
Meaning here, inflection there, stringing words as best he dare,
Hoping through the half-tuned muddle less than more will be his trouble.

On Speaking

To answer soundly people's questions wisdom will suffice,
Let minds be active, tongue obeying righteous sacrifice.
Have firm in thought your words to speak so others can perceive
What good you have to grace the world that others may not grieve.

On Songs

A song in the heart may arise and persist,
Defying strong efforts to alter its vein;
But if it be evil you must needs resist
Vain Babylon's trappings, let heaven's psalms reign.

Ecuador. *Even certain birds and animals are
capable of mimicking human languages,
besides possessing their own lingo.
Speaking and singing make society
function; without them it would be a drab
and very different world indeed.*

Things of Value, Reconstituting the Self

Breaking Carnal Nature

Man's carnal self, the stuff of dark deception,
Can ill be harnessed, thrust out, or ignored.
To kill its curse, its venomous corruption,
We rest in God, embrace our awesome Lord.

My heart craves to master the reins of this spirit,
Fighting these unsteady human devices
Constantly rearing their insults — I hear it —
Against righteous bulwarks that flourish in crisis.

No power exists which can counter the power
Of God's awesome purpose within us computed,
So to this great Spirit I bow low each hour
In humble remembrance of trials commuted.

Colombia. *Many people consider true wealth to be material things, such as gold, silver, houses, land, or automobiles, but these will all pass away in the course of time, leaving only eternal values in their wake: love, joy, peace patience, humility, faithfulness, and kindness that make life rich and meaningful.*

Things of Value, Reconstituting the Self

Fixing the Worst

Find the most offensive niche inside your humble home,
And fix it up to shine like new, as David's kingly throne.
There is no greater joy I see within our hard-spent days,
Than taking something fit for trash and making it worth praise.

Our Maker likewise sees in us such filthy works and lust
That He would just as soon disband His creatures to the dust …
But like the mind of His creations — built in Godly image —
So He loves to turn the worst of us to His own visage.

Objects of Value

I find myself walking along streambeds supple with stones, some few perhaps of value,
But I seldom stop any more to reach down and examine a possible specimen,
For as my years flee like a plover in flight,
So the truly valuable things this earth can offer are seldom seen.
Rather, they are sensed by the spirit, and dwell in heavenly places,
The means by which I rest peacefully upon the sea of glass,
Amidst the agates and crystals of unseen realms all around.

Hillsboro, Oregon. *Some of the most precious things on earth are agates and other rocks with their unique banding, colors, and designs, which are brought to light through careful cutting and polishing … just as our Creator chips away the ugliness of our character and polishes it to suit Himself.*

Tired and Fatigued

Chapter 24

Seeking Life

So often tired, not seldom weak,
Yet day by day the Lord I seek,
To lift a life whose selfish breath
Would lose itself in culture's death

Tired

Tired, yes, but not demoralized;
Weak, indeed, but free of conscience's pain;
In search of quiet solace, of a truth,
But never too dismayed to find restitution of spirit
Amidst the most hectic of life's fiery storms.

Sinai, South Dakota. *We all become tired at times, after working hard, perhaps experiencing a sleepless night, or are ill for a season. Then it is time to pull away from the cares of this world and look up into the heavens, and marvel at the great spectacles the Eternal places before us: a sunset, powerful storms, or the skillful flight of geese and butterflies. They will all rejuvenate and uplift the spirit.*

Suffering Through Trials

A Weight Too Heavy

At times the grievous burdens seem beyond my strength to bear,
Weights a-planted squarely on these shoulders; none are shed,
But bear them must this seeking child of clay amidst the glare
Of spotlights blazing ceaselessly upon this hoary head …

    Reflecting eternity's ransom,
    A life sacrificed that others may live.

Aging's Tests

As years fly by and age creeps in,
One never knows what grief, what sin
Might plague this finite child of clay …
But true as sunrise greets the day,
Some new affliction shall unfold
To humble pride … refine your gold.

Fiery Trials

When in fear the body quakes,
And harsh reward our poor soul takes;
Life's confusion seems to feed
Dark wrath upon our tender seed.

Know in truth complacency
Will stifle change to such degree
That useful vessels of your clay
Can He no longer dare display …

Continued on page 101

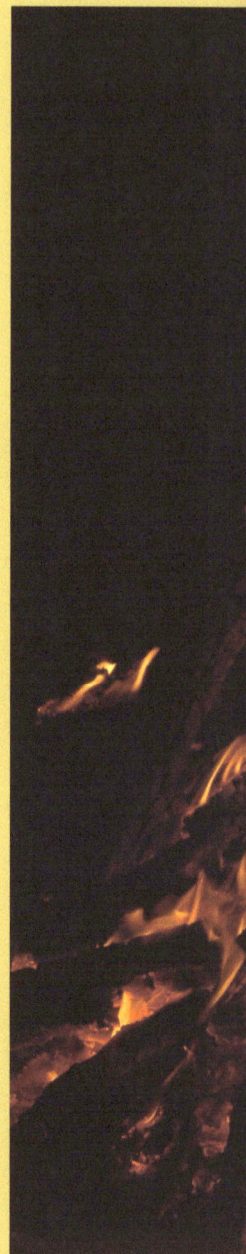

Pritchett, Texas.

Fiery trials are par for the course for those who choose the difficult and narrow pathway that leads to life. Though difficult, it leads to eternal life, and the fire is worth every bit of sweat and tears that might come upon us.

Galapagos Islands, Ecuador. *Sometimes sore trials place you in a lonely, barren desert without friends to support you, and death and destruction seem to surround you. You can be certain that the Adversary is behind this perversion of viewpoint, and you will come out of the trial a more refined and seasoned person.*

Continued from page 98

For all men tremble in God's hold —
Some gents of stubble, others gold.
Be sure in trials you drink His cup,
That fire refines … does not burn up.

Heaven's Microcosm

We live a microcosm of the heaven's lofty plan,
Each of us not knowing much of God's resplendent span
Of wisdom, bringing each creation through the strait and narrow
Paths of mercy to His throne, far from this world's dark peril.

Lift Me Up

Lift me up, great Creator in heaven.
Release me from the bonds of corruption in this world of death,
For I am deeply distressed.
Tears fall as rain from my eyes;
Sorrow engulfs me all around, and I yearn for Your salvation.
Cast my enemies far from me,
And open my understandings to Your wondrous works,
Your astounding creation and over-awesome goodness.
Lead me beside the still waters which Your spirit has lain within my bosom,
And grant me safe haven under the shelter of Your wings.

Suffering Through Trials

Lost

No place to hide ... no niche to cling ...

Sheep for the slaughter
Aswim in deep water,

Forsaking life's pride ... true love freely sing ...

Unfit for man's tenure,
Rejected indenture;

Eyes open wide ... towards heaven prayers ring ...

Teardrops as rain
Upon desert's stain;

Wistful souls tried ... full seasons may bring ...

Honey sipped sweetly,
Clear waters drunk deeply

On Pain and Suffering

My spirit moves forward toward great effort and accomplishment.
It ceases not to achieve the impossible, the difficult.
Should the risks merit the fruits of fulfilled dreams, Edenic wonderment,
Yet thoughts of brutal efforts towards achievement lead this one
Face to face with fleshly shortfalls, the spirit's oversight into misapprehensions,
The realization that agonies and sufferings must greet my efforts

Continued on page 103

Continued from page 102

Should thoughts of worth be carried forward into wisdom's accomplishments.
What a paradox:

> That which is good and lasting for man's self and his society
> Should be born through grief and suffering.

Is it not the footsteps of the sons of God which have shown us
That indeed lawlessness has enforced upon a sinful world its truth,
Inherent upon physical realms of error, seas of discontent,
That through worlds of death must come blood sacrifices,
For without shed blood and bruised bodies there can be no atonement for sin,
And without bruising and crucifying the flesh one cannot see Eden,
The hope of mankind.

Preparation

Our lives, events, and daily fare prepare us for the fateful days
That test our constitution sore, expose our greatest weaknesses.
We know not when our trusted Master shall release harsh trials and frays
Upon us fragile vessels, sculptured deftly through tests' fastnesses.

Pulls of the World

Caught among the evil throes of Satan's lust-sick world,
The saints stand out a spectacle, their righteous stripes unfurled.

Yet no one views the royal battle deep within the heart,
Of called-out warriors holding fast God's dreams — them not depart.

Continued on page 104

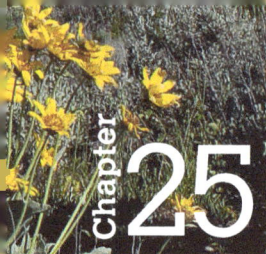

Suffering Through Trials

Continued from page 103

The battle rages ceaselessly, in waves of troops a-ready,
In wait, attacking, hiding, Satan's army none-too-steady.

This world of Lucifer's assault creeps in from every crack
Of his vain-ordered world of death, of lustful fleeting lack

Embedded in the fabric of this cosmos he designed,
Enticing men to worship him, and to his quests resign.

Amidst the furious battle raging for the minds of men,
Was ever there a question how this skirmish sore should end?

Indeed implanted in the soul God's mind itself shall reign,
Within His saints, the fulcrum for earth's kingdom He has lain.

And from the ancient times He knew we all would purchased be,
Within His Realm, each day rejecting pride and vanity.

Suffering

Throughout this life of stress and pain
Accept your suffering course as gain,
For should there cease all grief and strife
You could not reap eternal life.
Harsh dues we pay through these short days;
Unmeasured realms our God repays.

Jackson Hole, Wyoming. By fastening your gaze upon the heavenly mountain of the Eternal — His seat of government — the suffering of manifold trials is placed in its proper perspective, and the pain becomes more bearable as the trial is seen for what it really is: a means to change you to become more like Him.

25 Suffering Through Trials

That Sneaky Feeling

Has ever your reasoning cranium thought perhaps as toils wear on,
While trials harsh and heartaches longingly punish love's sweet song,
That someone somewhere is sweetly nudging a lesson in under the door,
To calm you, cheer you, and ultimately lift you higher than before?

That We May Produce

Fraught with continual suffering I stand
Naked and bare holding God's ageless hand.
I ask that the pain be diminished, but nay,
No sooner I ask than yet other trials play
Upon the fair meadows of life's vaporous fling,
Bidding I humble this flesh 'midst life's sting.

We ought not request that the pain go away,
For only through trials can sharp edges sway
Our pathway aright so our works may complete
The Maker's bright secrets He planted discrete
And surely within fleshly vessels He sought,
This haven of secrets the Father's will brought.

Yellowstone National Park, Wyoming. *Water will quench fire, but water itself can become so hot that it will scald your flesh. We must respect its symbolism as the spirit of the Creator and the universal solvent for living cells and blood to sustain life, but not forget its sterilizing power when heated to the boiling point.*

Troubles

If troubles multiply and they
Submerge and cast your hopes away,
Step back a moment, think and listen
To the spirit dreams that glisten
Bright as our great God has planned;
Trials shall pass, in strength you'll stand

Thorns

Swept up in pride the saint is stung
With barbs and thorns to humble him;
Like Paul we pray that thorns be flung
Far from our selves as unclean things.

Our Savior will extend His grace
In ways beyond our fondest schemes
To bring us to that wondrous place …
The Holy City … consummate dreams.

Pritchett, Texas.

The end result of bearing through trials is to become a better and purer individual, tried in the fire and, like a flower of the forest or field, more attractive to the Creator who is the One who will pull you out of the flames.

Life's Mission

I never felt the pure, brisk breeze of God's new morning,
Saw the brilliant, golden sunset reflecting Zion's tiered heights,
Heard the flitting warblers amidst the spray of thundering falls,
Felt the warmth of home's flaming hearth amidst family's loving circle,
Smelled the deep purple of lilacs upon cool earth's passionate fragrance,
Or tasted summer's rich fruit of life beside bubbling brooks,
Nor sensed true mission and fullness of purpose,
    pure liberty and freedom of highest intent —
Until I knew what God meant when He said, "Follow Me," instead of mere men.

Man's Ceaseless Dreams

On and on roll the days of man's misfortune.
Methodically he reaches for windfalls from vanity's ripe trees,
And seldom recounts how willfully he trod asunder the spotless hopes of the guiltless.
Onward stumble dreams and miscalculations,
	the heavy burdens of torment from lack of truth.
Insidiously the days come and go, all pointing towards the darkness of the grave.
Schemes bud, grow, and dissipate to leave but dried splinters where once grew a hearty,
	mighty forest giant, spreading upward and outward ... only to cease abruptly
	within its brightest days.

On and on roll the days of man's misfortune.
Few discover the utter purpose of unfolding days, but reserve knowledge for darkness,
	and exchange humility for pride.
Yet, worms cover the short days of venture to forever seal the end of all flesh,
And judgment forgets her abiding place, for she is given no berth and is forgotten.
On and on roll the schemes, with lessons learned but man's ultimate end
	seldom contemplated.

No Place to Hide

You cannot hide your deeds in darkness,
Light will shine someday and publish
Every secret, motives foolish,
Shouting forth your works in sharpness.

Juneau, Alaska. *Sitting in front of a powerful, cascading waterfall can do little else but envigorate the spirit and direct one's thoughts toward the power of the creation behind all that is.*

Understanding Life

On Slavery

I am but a slave, a poor one no less,
Though not a ring in my nose, should I bless
The day that you enter the earth for to rest,
And I in my freedom deny the request
You put in your will … that I remain still,
That when you should leave this world I would not thrill
At the thought of my freedom you've not given me;
Oh, pity that master whose wealth is not free.

Perplexity

Doldrums of emptiness sweep deftly across my soul,
Without fanfare, without bluster … so calmly sent.
This soldier of many battles drinks in of perplexity
Upon the castletop hill of pure-blue, crystal firmaments,
Unconscious of meanings too deep to fathom,
Unclear of pathways too faint to discern,
Just lying on cool earth, staring into blue-sweeping space,
Searching for beginnings of endeavors sorely needed,
Plottings powerfully perceived but left in doubt
By this world's confusion and darkness;
Bodies, hearts, and minds purchased from loss
But blunted — for a short season — by unforeseen apathy,
That silent resident that sometimes shares its vagrancy with me.

Sinai, South Dakota. *A young robin growing rapidly to an adult in a mere few weeks gives encouragement to the thought that we also may grow up quickly in the truths of life that are fed to us by the awesome creation all around us, I which we ought to surround ourselves.*

Purpose

All things in their time do swiftly
Extend their sweet influences deftly,
To spring traps among men less knowing,
That God's grandest purpose be showing.

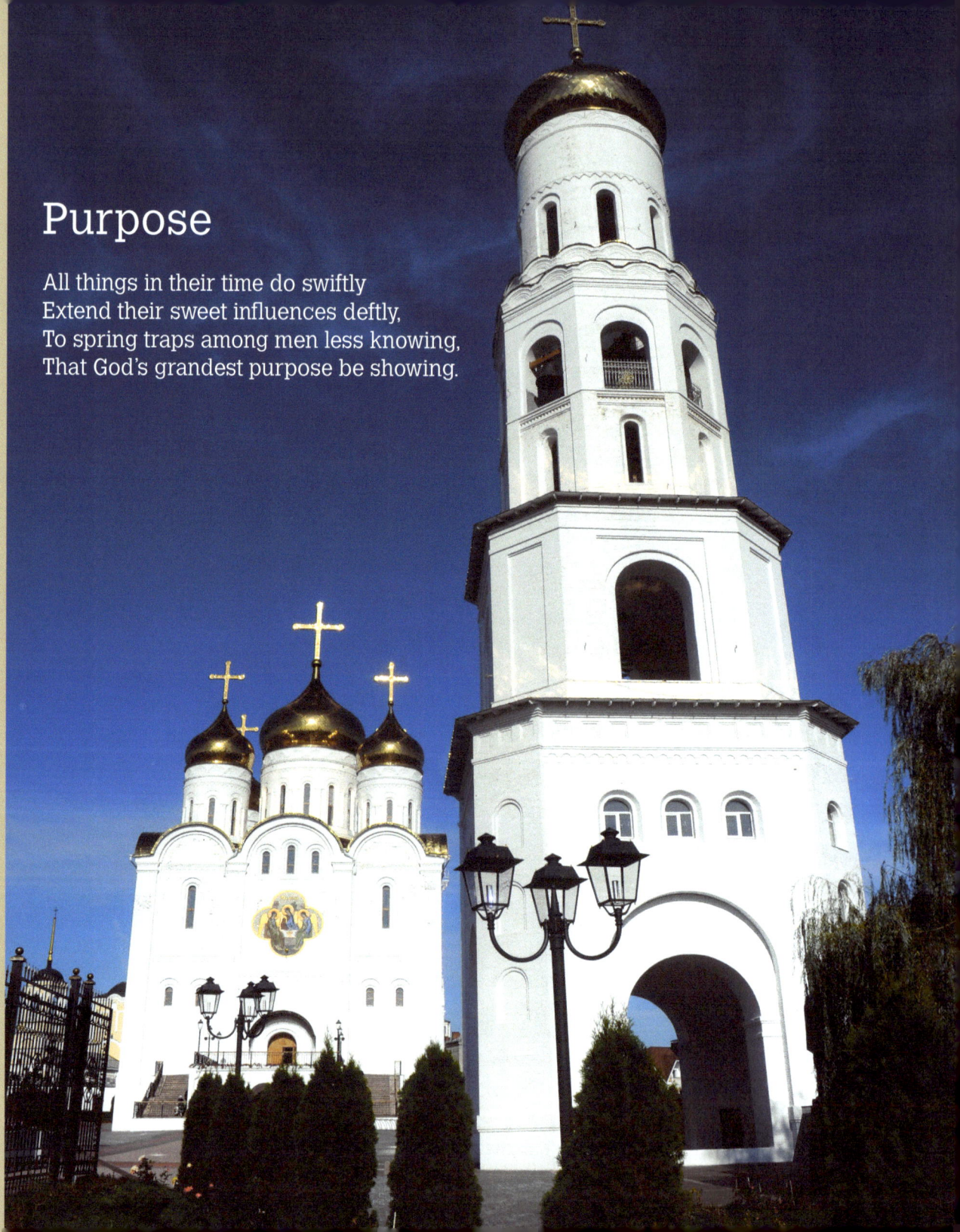

Reality

Quest for reality, minds of searching savants,
Grasping for truth amidst mankind's deception,
Hurling the masses along the wide, easy pathways
Into uneasy existence, confused minds and hearts,
Forsaking basic truths hidden for ages and generations
That stare squarely into the face of searching hearts …
The strait and narrow way of truth,
God's gift of reality, the I AM,
That I also may be … in the Savior's footsteps.

Seeking Self

I saw the image of the man, painted as I ought to be,
But lo, my self could not stretch forth, embrace this image I could see
So deftly painted by the people touted for their wisdom great;
My self tried desperately to mold into the kind they celebrate.

Though taught to hate the man I am, yet is that view of me God-sent?
The conflict raged within my heart: who wins this war of brutal bent?
Should images of men hold sway, and rule the day while injured pray
That what we are — creation's clay — ought be the Maker's will replay?

There was no challenge, all was clear, I had to leave the false façade,
And form God's creature made in fear … to find him 'midst world's mad charade.

Kiev. Ukraine. *The beginning and the end of life ought to be on the minds of all of us as we strive to understand what our purpose in life is, where we came from, and where we are going once this present physical life is past. After all, we will all die in the flesh and ought to grasp these basic truths before that time.*

Chapter 26

Understanding Life

The Course Not Seen

So often we do not understand the winding road we walk,
Strait and narrow through murky bogs and over quaking sands,
Down dim primeval forest paths, or through blinding blizzards …
Until those crises around us clear for a moment,
And in amazement we see and perceive, as from a distance
The fray which engulfed us in mystery and confusion
For a season of grief and testing, that entwined us with a battle
We could not perceive — too close it clung to us.
Ought not we in humble gratitude
Thank the One whose great love thought us worthy
To tip-toe towards perfection just one bit more
Through trials He set before us?

The End of Dreams

Man may build many a dream, scheme many a scheme,
But unless he builds that dream or scheme on the wisdom of the Creator,
He fails in his quests, and falls into ignominy at the end of days
When all affairs of men meet their just reward.

Porter, Minnesota. *It does the soul good to contemplate the fact that we will someday pass from the land of the living and enter the grave, then turn back to the elements from which we came. While death is an enemy, it cannot be victorious over the resurrection of those sleeping in the grave, and ought to spur everyone on to accomplish worthwhile goals while still amongst the living.*

Chapter 26

What Is Life

What is this life?
I strive to overcome, and master the tongue,
But shame overtakes me.
I try to live by eternal words,
But perfection eludes me.
My hopes lead ever towards releasing guilt,
But fear and doubts plague me.
What is this life?
How impotent I see myself as a child of clay,
But how great is the Advocate of all men through all time,
Who made this amazing creature called man in His image,
And changes us with a lively hope that is never dampened.

You Know Not the Day

You know not the day's gifts to you,
Oh man of childish clay,
For morn may grant the joy of ease
But evening great dismay.

South Dakota. *Wisps of cirrus clouds draw one's gaze upwards towards heaven, the dwelling place of the Creator, who gives meaning and understanding to life because He made all that is. It pays to heed His voice if one is interested in life beyond the grave... and that includes all of us.*

Sorting Words

People babble aimlessly amid a din of words,
While priceless platitudes lie buried, scarcely to be heard.

Men are known by words they choose, for better or for worse,
And rare the man who deftly sorts the blessing from the curse.

Words

Words …

> Revelators of the heart's intent,
> Keepers of sage's dark secrets,
> Directors of nations and peoples,
> Protectors of life and harbingers of death …

Yet elude perfection's hungry conquests
Within my anguished, foolish tongue,
Its gesticulations searching frantically for truth,
But out blurts vanity when kindness should reign.

Continued on page 123

Viet Nam. *Sometimes words need not be spoken at all to get across a powerful message, especially when there exists a language barrier. The reticent man may be considered wise if he keeps his mouth shut even though he may be a fool.*

Dear Children,
Today is a bright day here in the
South *is a* Sonata *of*
the woods
birds

Continued from page 121

Try as one might perfection eludes the grasp;
It ever seeks its will, yet never finds it.
Slippery and elusive its toilsome fulfillment slips away …
And I stand naked and accused,
My tongue cleaving to my mouth in pain.

Utter, despicable instrument of pain that it is
This reflector of human nature's vile spirit
Wreaks anguish upon my spirit,
As upward I strive, ever checked by false step's Guide,
Ever wary of my Wilderness Guide's ways.

Words of Tired Souls

I know not why these words so sigh when flesh is drained of zeal,
When day wears deep and rest dawns sweet in vivid contemplation.

So swiftly said these words ought tend to kind refrains that heal,
But opt instead to rear their head 'midst thorns and denigration.

Oh yes, I know, that fetid field which wrath so often doles;
Tis but the fruit of tired minds, not love for bleeding souls.

Sinai, South Dakota. *Words have power! They move people, families, and nations, enable civilization to move forward, and define cultures around the world. Language is built into the very fabric of the human species, made in the image of God, and the Word of God provides the platform for the Eternal's speaking to His created beings..*

Not of This Age

I have done so very little in this world,
Upset so few memorials of this present Babylon,
Perfected so few talents in the pursuit of the sublime,
And shall be known by so few in a world of billions.
One day soon I shall be but a memory, reality stultified and stilled, these atoms returning to the dust.
Yet fruits of the evil ones shall be remembered by the gods of the land, and vaunted by the masses.
For such a fate of obscurity I am not afraid, but shall one day beyond the realm of this eon
See the unrepentant hedonists cry in agony for a sip of my water …
But I shall not give them a drink,
For I cannot, nor am able to resurrect of my own power the hopes of the lost,
Who fling justice and mercy far from the lands of hope and praise,
And rest their trust in this age's mysteries.

Worth

To spend my days in worthy exploits, so my conscience yearns,
For why exist except that days in rich rewards returns
That will of zealous harmony with God's great plan unfurled,
Amidst the storied chaos that the Adversary's hurled.

Life is indeed one long-sought quest of seeking worthy hire,
While passing through this frothing sea, this agonizing fire,
Where no one stops to wipe the tears of heartache from your eyes,
Nor turns to seek the origin of agonizing cries. *Continued on page 126*

Arches arch. Arches National Park, Utah. *Having both feet firmly on the ground is essential when examining one's worth. Without a firm foundation anchored to the truth of the Creator, it is impossible to arrive at the right answers concerning the big questions of life: Why are you here, what is your purpose here, and where are you going?*

Continued from page 125

The weeks and months, short years of passion quickly swept aside
By sweat and toil of daily sacrifices fitly tried,
That somewhere, somehow through the fog of God's majestic plan
We yet may see our stately worth, His complementing hand.

Creator's Measure

I am older now, but once I was young.
Yet, whether old or young the same battle has raged:

What is my worth? Do I measure up?

No answer to this age-old questioning emerges easily,
But through the Creator's mind …
Who grants the bits of hope amidst today's depravity,
The earnest of worth transcending the wildest of dreams.

More Than a Worm

In this lone body I feel no grandeur,
The worm that I am … that is truth, I fear,
Though often it seems that others appraise
My worth far above my own inward gaze.

Perhaps that's the reason this place rests in peace,
My wife, kids, and cattle in joyful increase,
For ne'er do I think of this flesh being great;
I let God uplift me, His will my own fate.

Guatemala. *Understanding one's inner worth requires experience in life, as well as a firm attachment to the creation that the Creator has placed all around us. The farmer who produces the fruit of the field is very likely to have this attachment, and will be fulfilled in his or her everyday living.*

Peeking At Worth

Our fears so subtly tug at soul's
Incessant journey so divine,
To prove the self's untarnished goals
Grant worth and morrow's hope sublime.

We dare not peer and peek too far
Beyond our humble fleshly fort,
For should by chance we see life's star
That worth would surely flee its court.

Worthy Being

Oh, the over-awesome quest of man
To confirm his worth, to be rendered acceptable.
Over such endeavors will he traverse continents,
Expose his flesh and mind to untold suffering,
Lay down his life amidst the whims of exploits
To reveal to himself — and to that abstract world around him —
That he deserves to exist, to be here …
Questions that the Eternal has already answered …
Man the "I AM" to be.

Sinai, South Dakota. *There is nothing of greater value in this physical life than one's spouse, the wife for whom the husband would die for, and the husband for whom the wife pledges her allegiance to, that the two may grow together in love and joy as long as they live. Such worth is a picture of the love and headship in the spirit realm that is a mystery beyond human comprehension.*

Chapter 29

Writing

Born to Write

This hand must write; it was born to reach out from a mind crying to cast its bread upon the waters … to instruct the world in a better way, a way the Eternal has taught me, that wisdom which cries out within my humble breast. These words cannot be contained. They burn within me in a most profound fire of gratitude to my Creator, to the One whose pen must fashion my grip, express its nature upon tablets of gold from heaven's almighty fortresses.

Suppress this hand and this spirit must sink
To the pit of destruction where no soul may think,
Nor conjure up worlds fitly framed out of time,
Beyond current heartache and lost paradigm.

Do Not Add to ….

Oh, great challenges of strong endeavor's rhyme,
To gather stirring challenges in words sublime …
Yet never treading on declarations Divine,
Not adding to God's diction, let few jots be mine.

The Writer

The writer, steeped in personal quandaries yearning to unfold
The vagaries of heavy burdens placed upon his soul,
Seeks to unload them and draw converts to his realm,
To immortalize truths he holds dear — or deceptions for the wicked —
Transcending time, that his humble existence
Might yet prove worthy of each tedious breath and word.

Pritchett, Texas. *As the spider deftly weaves its web to catch its food, so the writer reaches out his net to snare knowledge from whatever source might provide it, and assembles that knowledge into a coherent pattern for others to read and digest. For those whose hand is so inclined it is a necessary part of life, which, if withheld, leaves a void that can only be filled by writing some more.*

Why I Write

A writer indeed I must be,
But putting away fairy tales
Let this fertile imagination ring forth the fancy of sages,
And spring forth the wisdom of ages and generations
Heaped upon men yearning for truth,
To bequeath knowledge and understanding
That my children's children may gain an inheritance.

Write I Must!

Write, write, this pen longs to write,
Perhaps to accomplish, see pages done, like so many corn rows planted and hoed;
Or maybe to see my worth, transcend time and bequeath a legacy of ideals to my
    children and grandchildren.
Whatever the truth I do not know,
But one thing I do know: I must write!
These fingertips burn to reveal the mysteries so few have been invited to see ...
    or touch ... or hear.
I long to record them ... or create them;
Sometimes the purpose is obscure, but nevertheless
Write I must, for that is me!

www.ingramcontent.com/pod-product-compliance
Lightning Source LLC
Chambersburg PA
CBHW042012090426

42811CB00015B/1622

* 9 7 8 0 9 9 9 8 0 2 5 4 5 2 *